Anti-Stress Dot-to-Dot

Emily Wallis is an illustrator who uses traditional hand-drawn techniques. She completed her MA in Sequential Design and Illustration at the University of Brighton. Her clients include Scholastic, *Jamie Magazine*, and Quarto Publishing.

Also by Emily Wallis

The Silver Pony Ranch series
by D.L. Green, illustrated by Emily Wallis

Emily Wallis

Anti-Stress Dot-to-Dot

Beautiful, calming pictures to complete yourself

BOXTREE

First published 2015 by Boxtree
an imprint of Pan Macmillan
20 New Wharf Road, London N1 9RR
Associated companies throughout the world
www.panmacmillan.com

ISBN 978-0-7522-6586-5

3 5 7 9 8 6 4

A CIP catalogue record for this book is available from the British Library.

Printed and bound in Italy by Printer Trento S.r.l.

Visit **www.panmacmillan.com** to read more about all our books
and to buy them. You will also find features, author interviews and
news of any author events, and you can sign up for e-newsletters
so that you're always first to hear about our new releases.

Nowadays, it can be hard to find time to remove ourselves from the scramble of modern life and truly relax. Working with your hands is one of the best ways to clear your mind and what better way to do this than the timeless pleasure of dot-to-dot? Let the day's worries slip away as you focus on gradually revealing the picture in front of you, number by number. It's a simple enough activity, yet the charm of the pictures you uncover will delight you.

This book is small enough to fit in your bag and big enough to offer a satisfying feeling of accomplishment once you've finished. Each picture will take around fifteen minutes to complete. Don't worry too much about hitting the dots precisely, and don't panic if you make a mistake – one missed line won't ruin the overall picture. Be mindful of the pen in your hand and the emerging image in front of you as the rhythm of connecting the numbers begins to soothe you.

Once you have your eye in, you might want to think of ways to personalize the drawings, perhaps by roughly sketching the lines with pencil, or working more precisely with an ink pen. Different methods will offer a slightly different result every time. You might even choose to colour the pictures in once you've finished. Each drawing offers a new opportunity to be creative.

Whatever your method and wherever you take your book, we hope that you enjoy taking a moment out of your day with these beautiful dot-to-dot pictures.

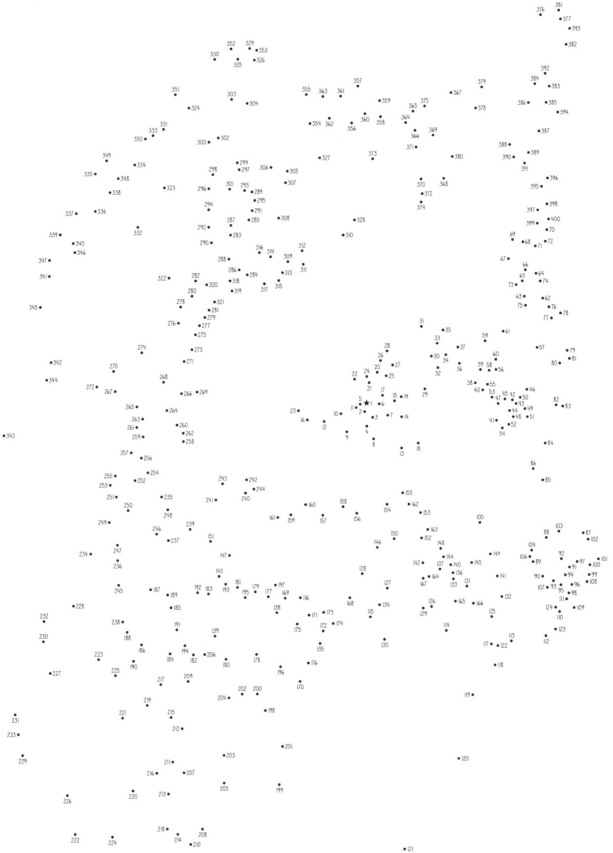

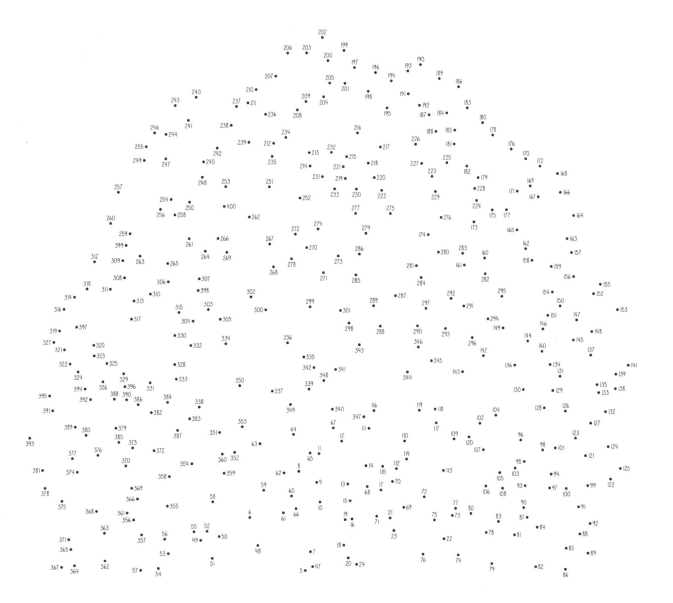

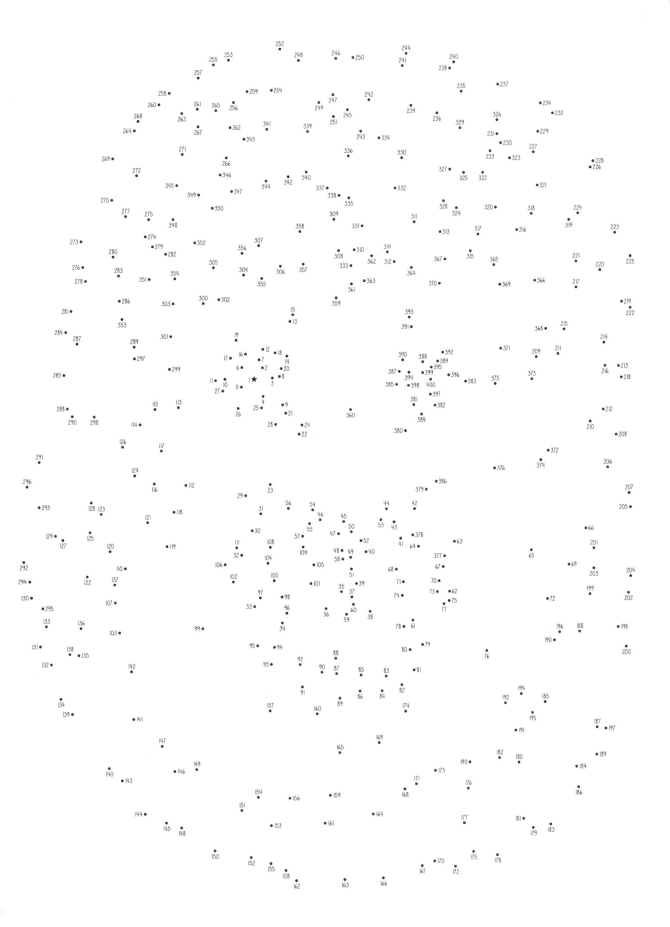

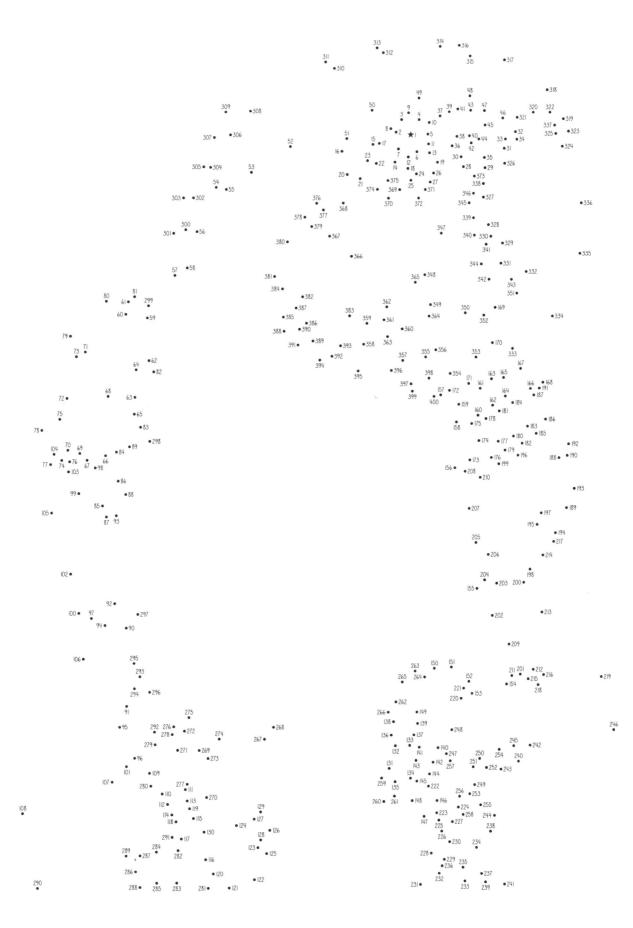

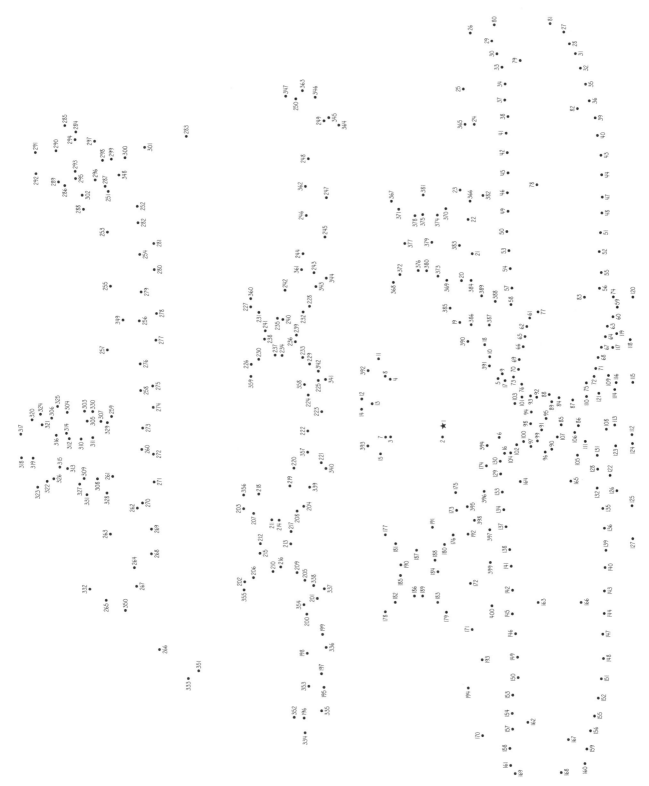

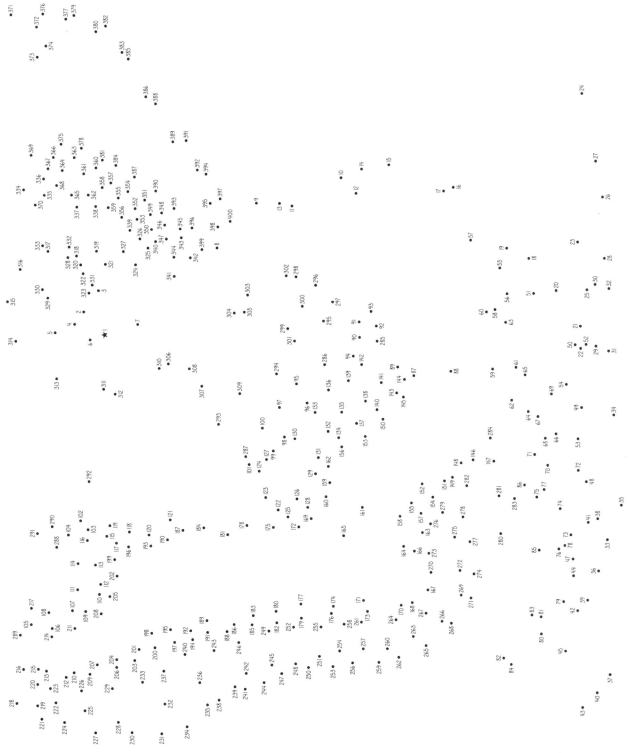

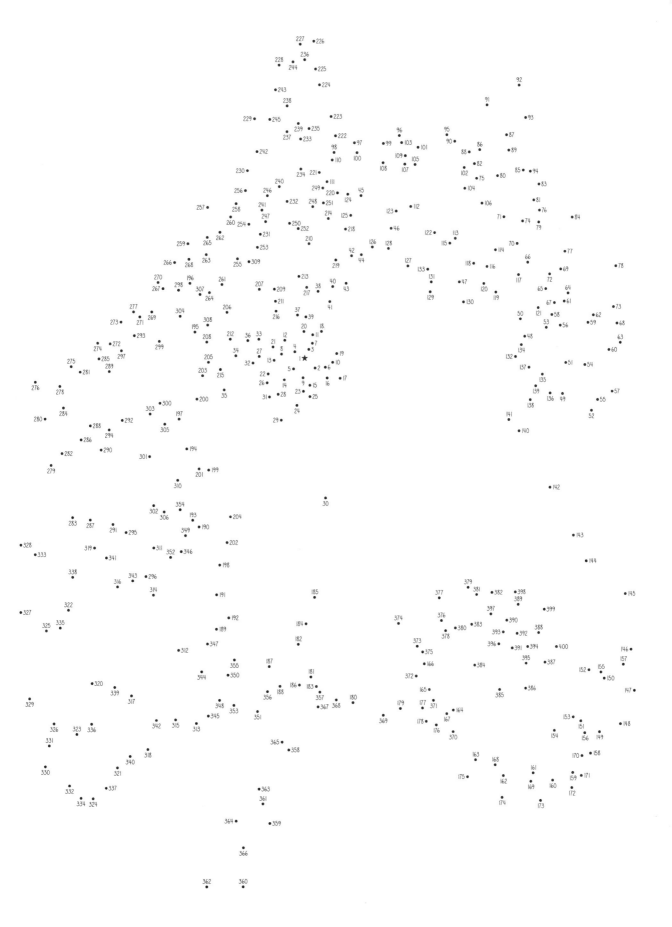

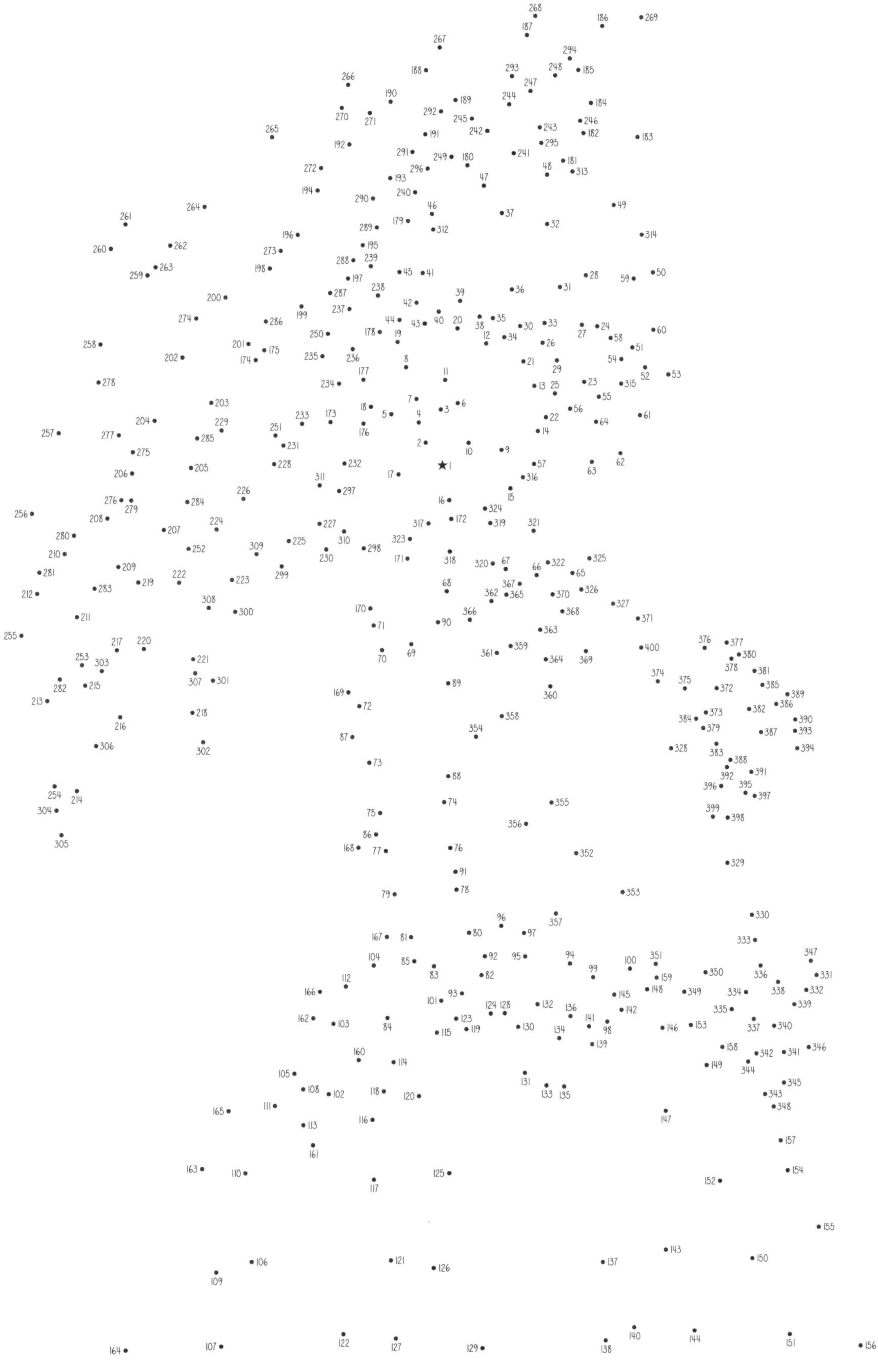

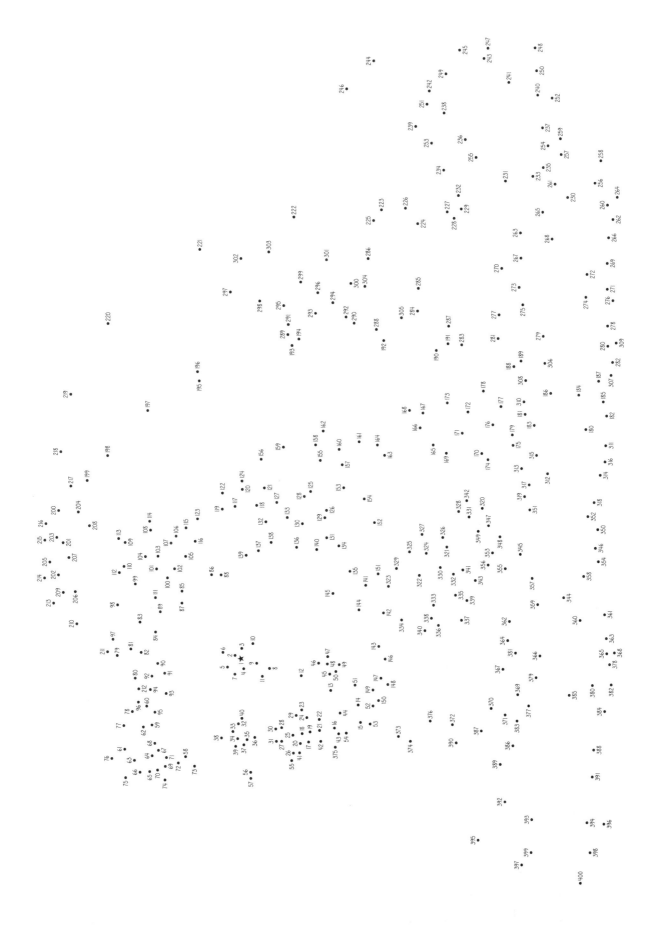

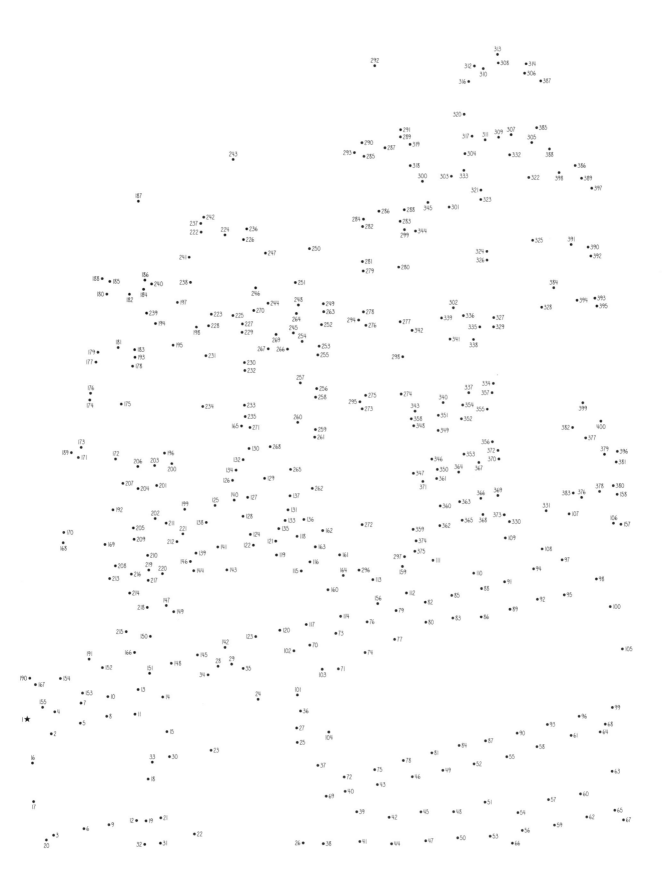

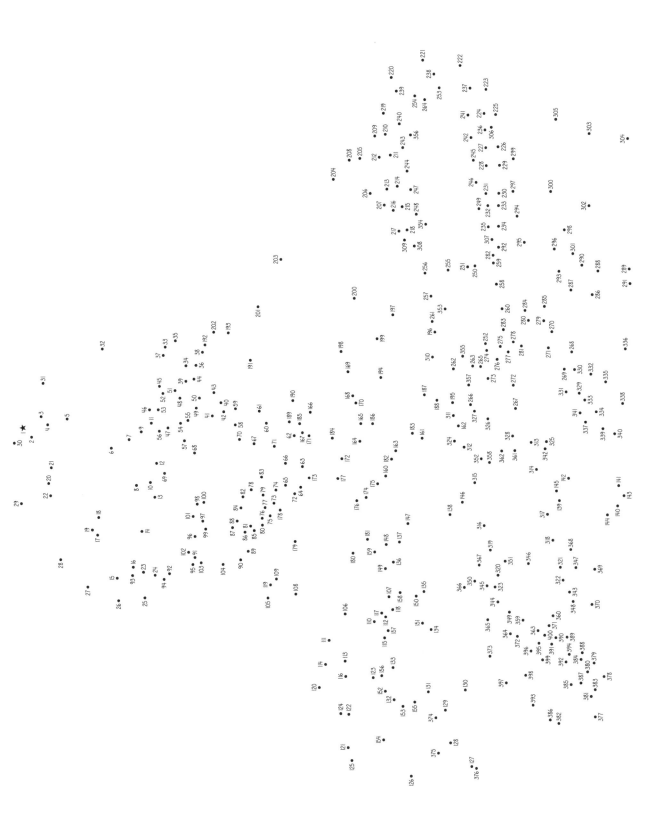

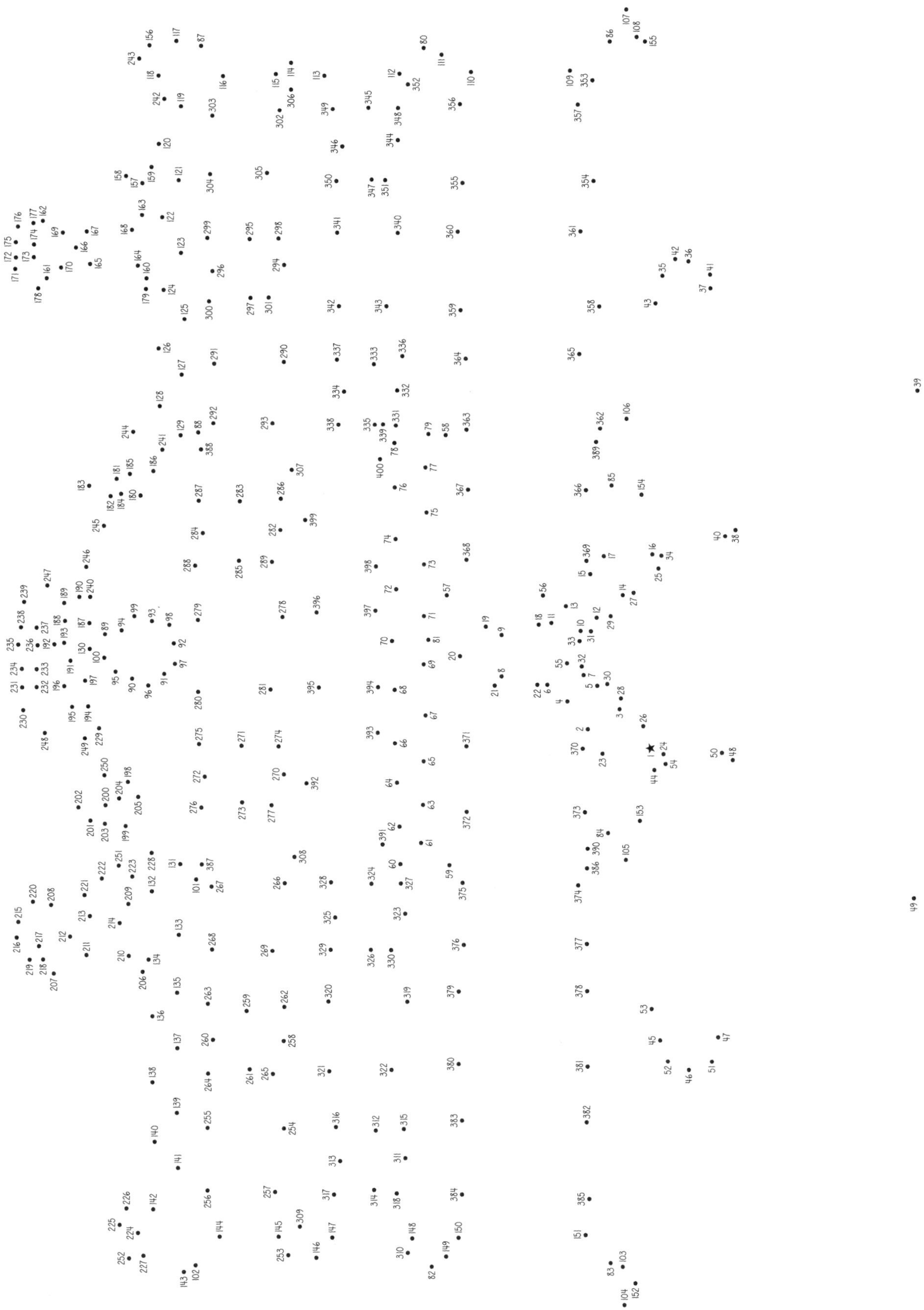

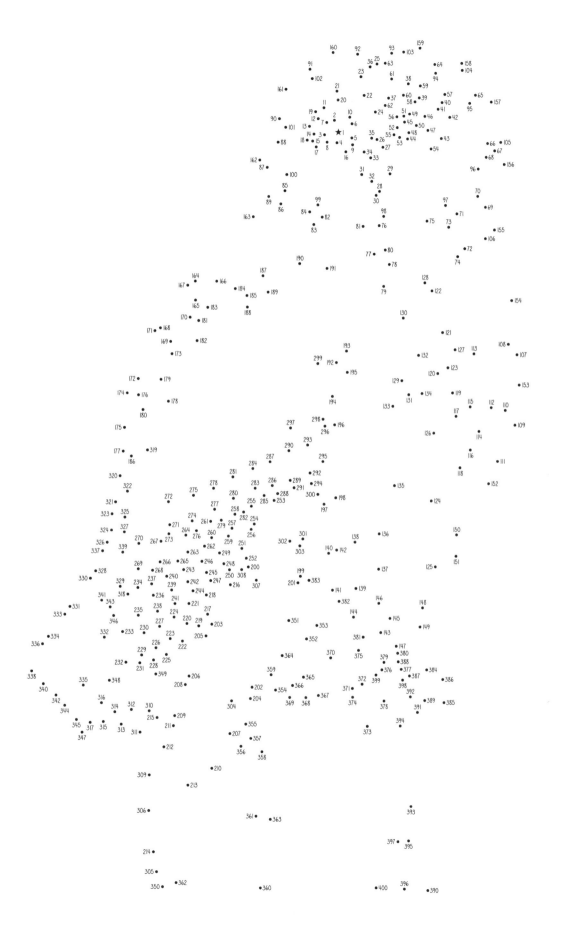

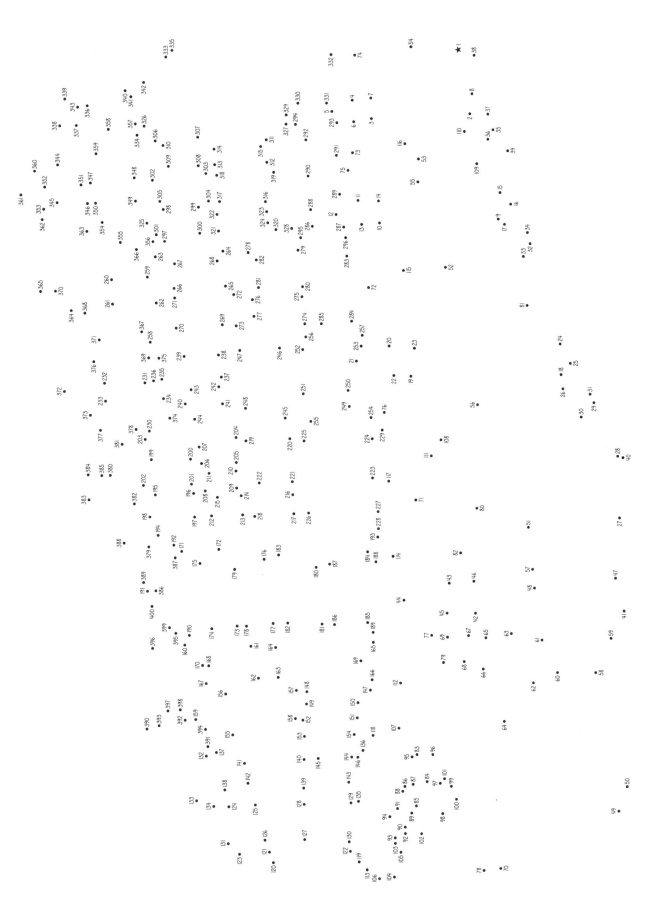

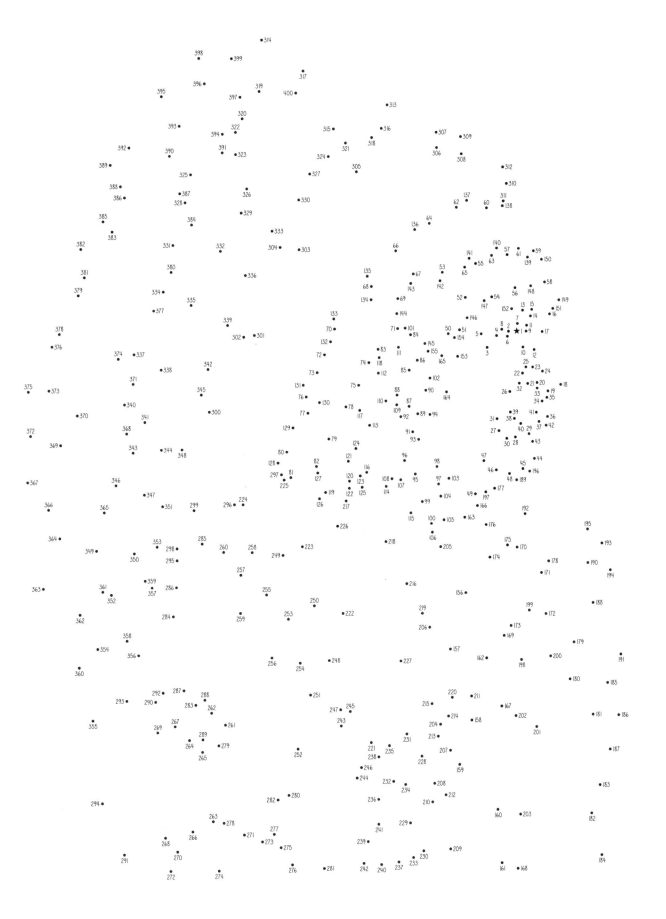

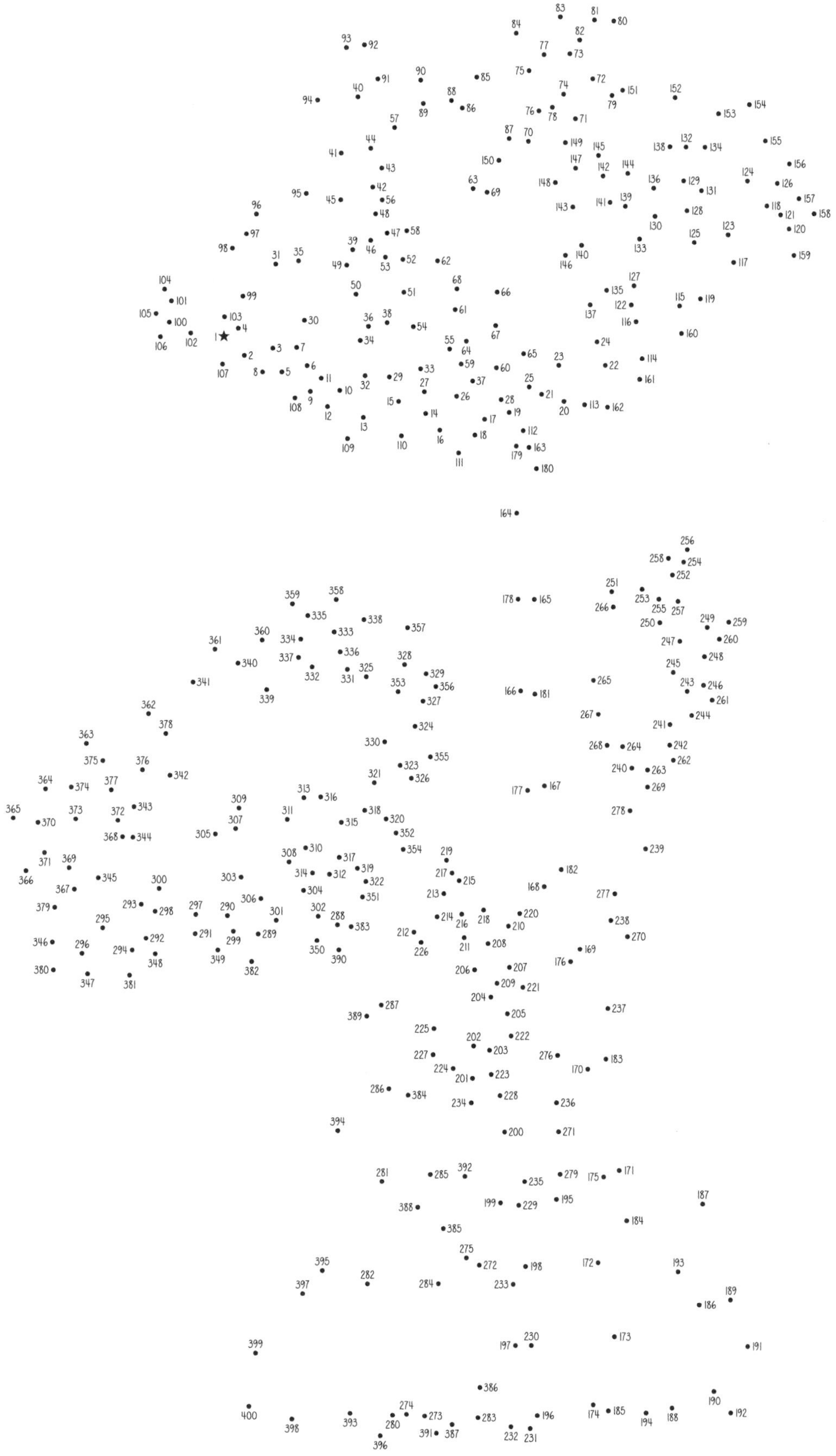

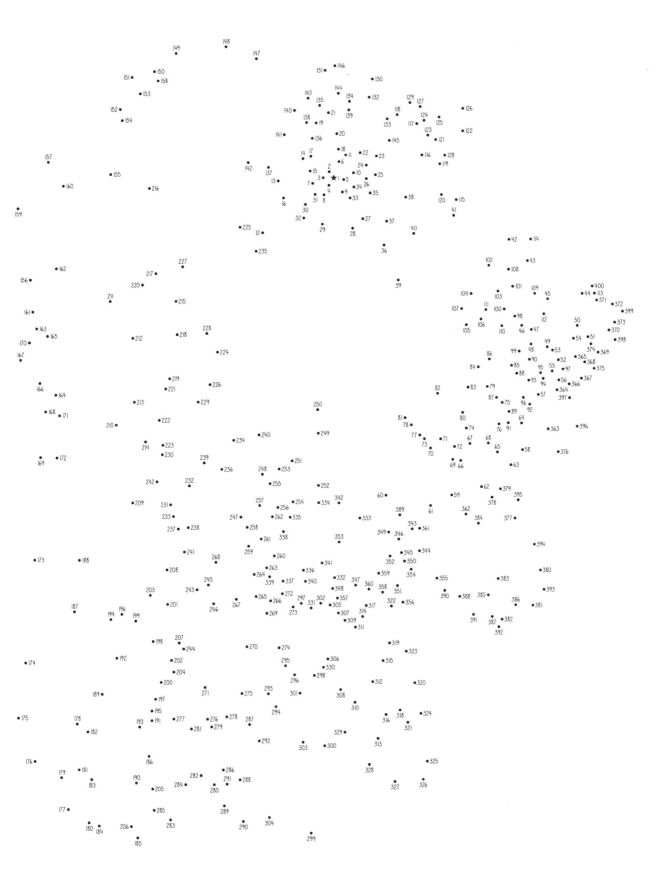

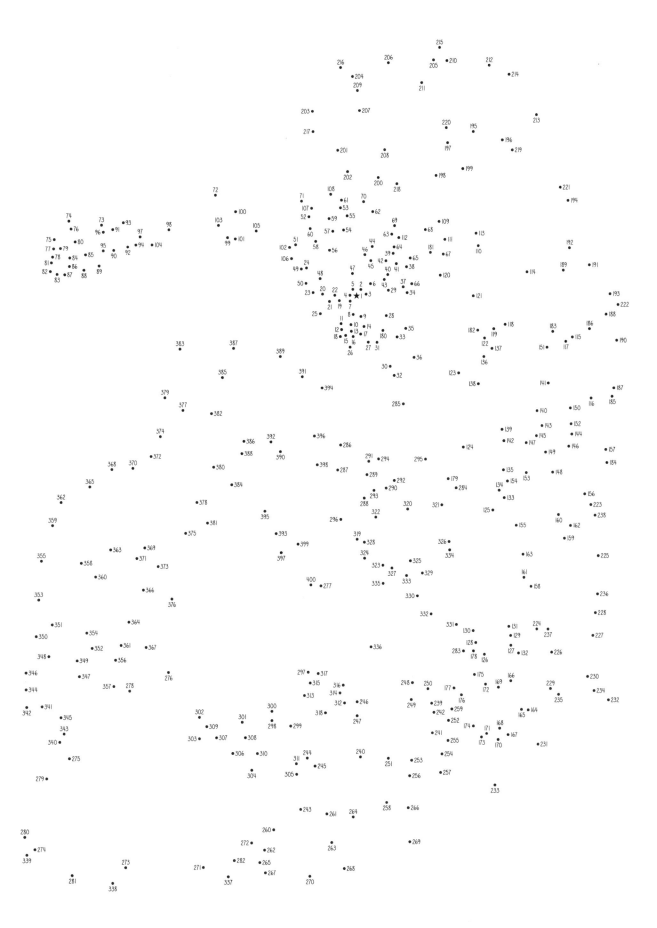

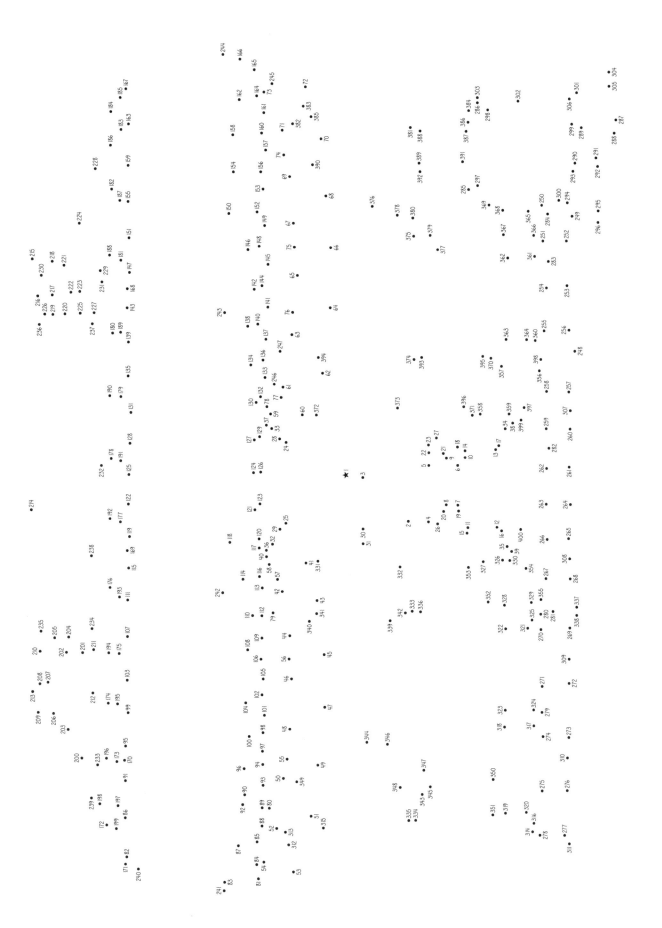

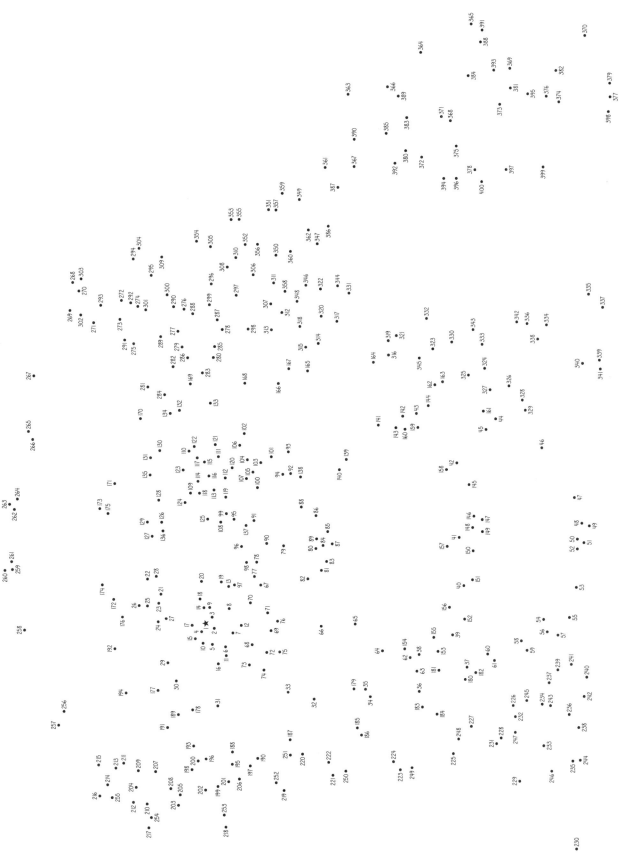

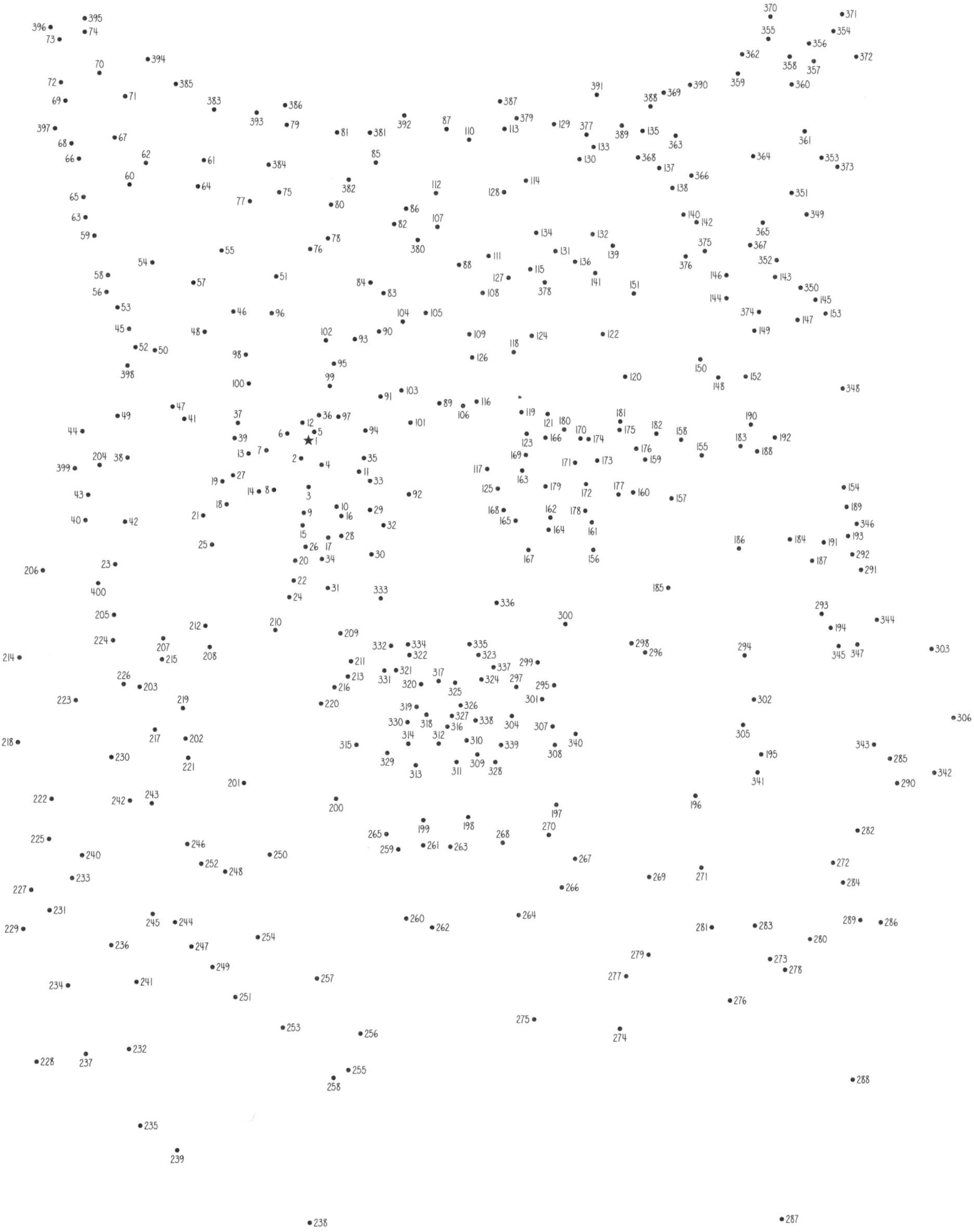

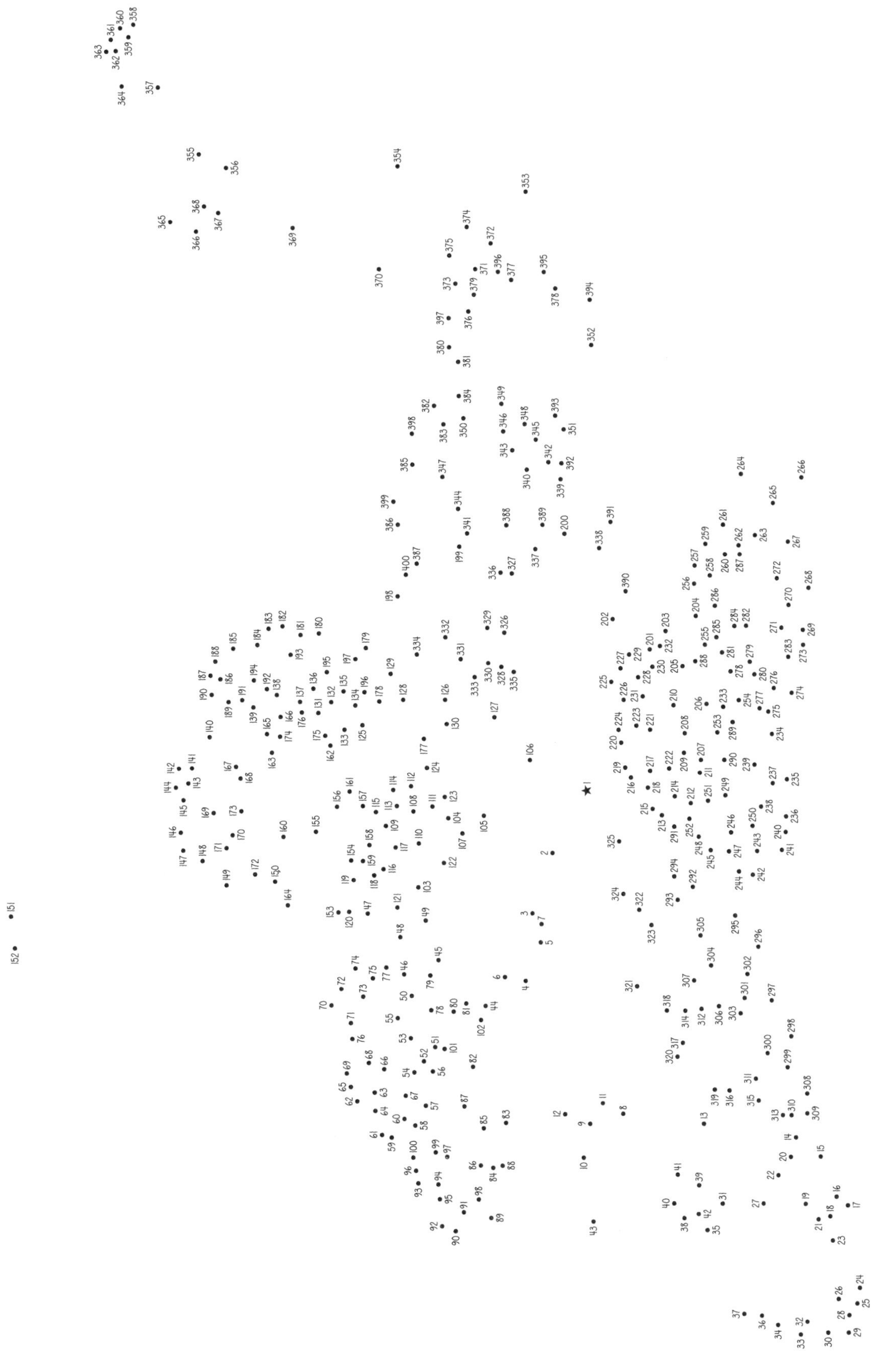

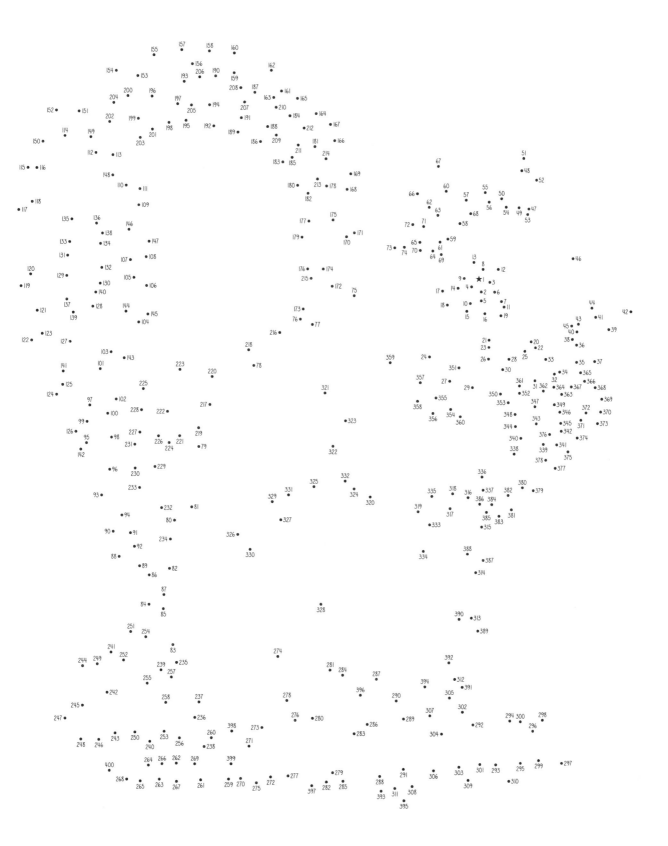

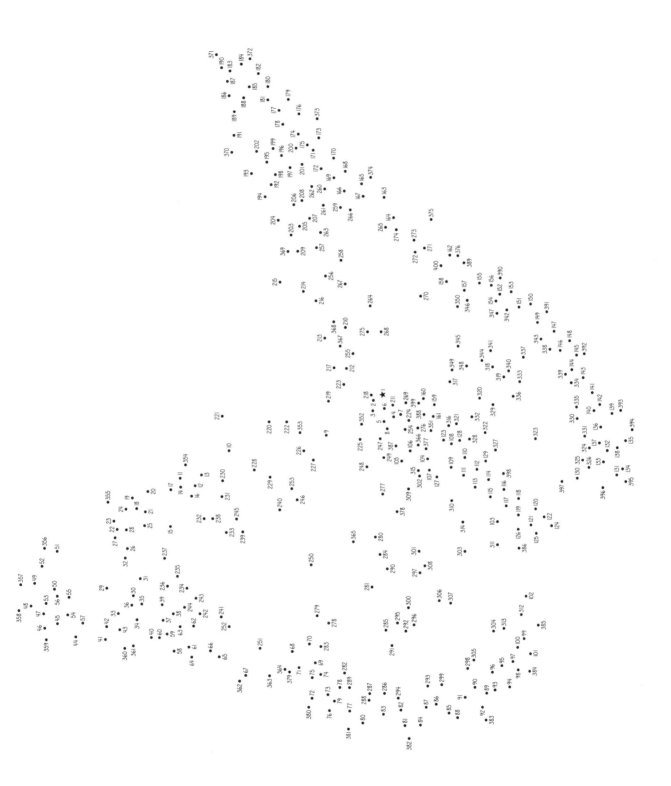

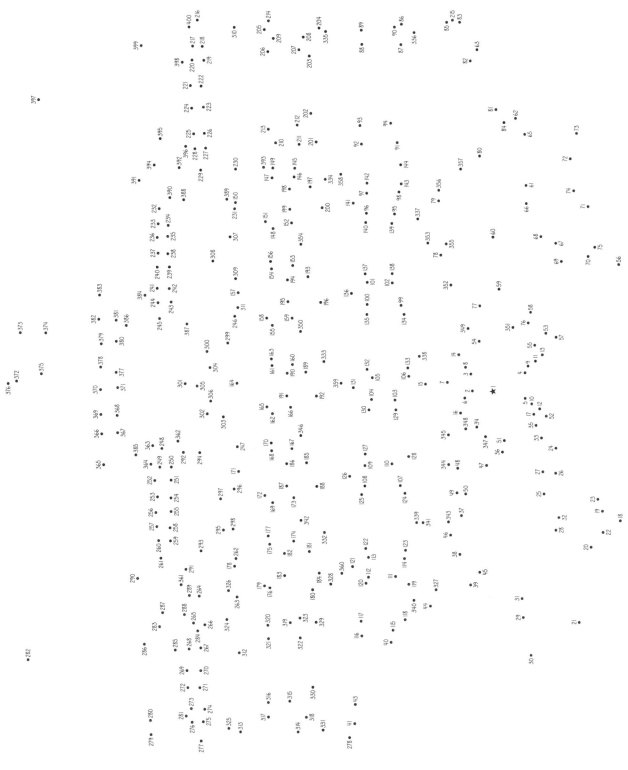

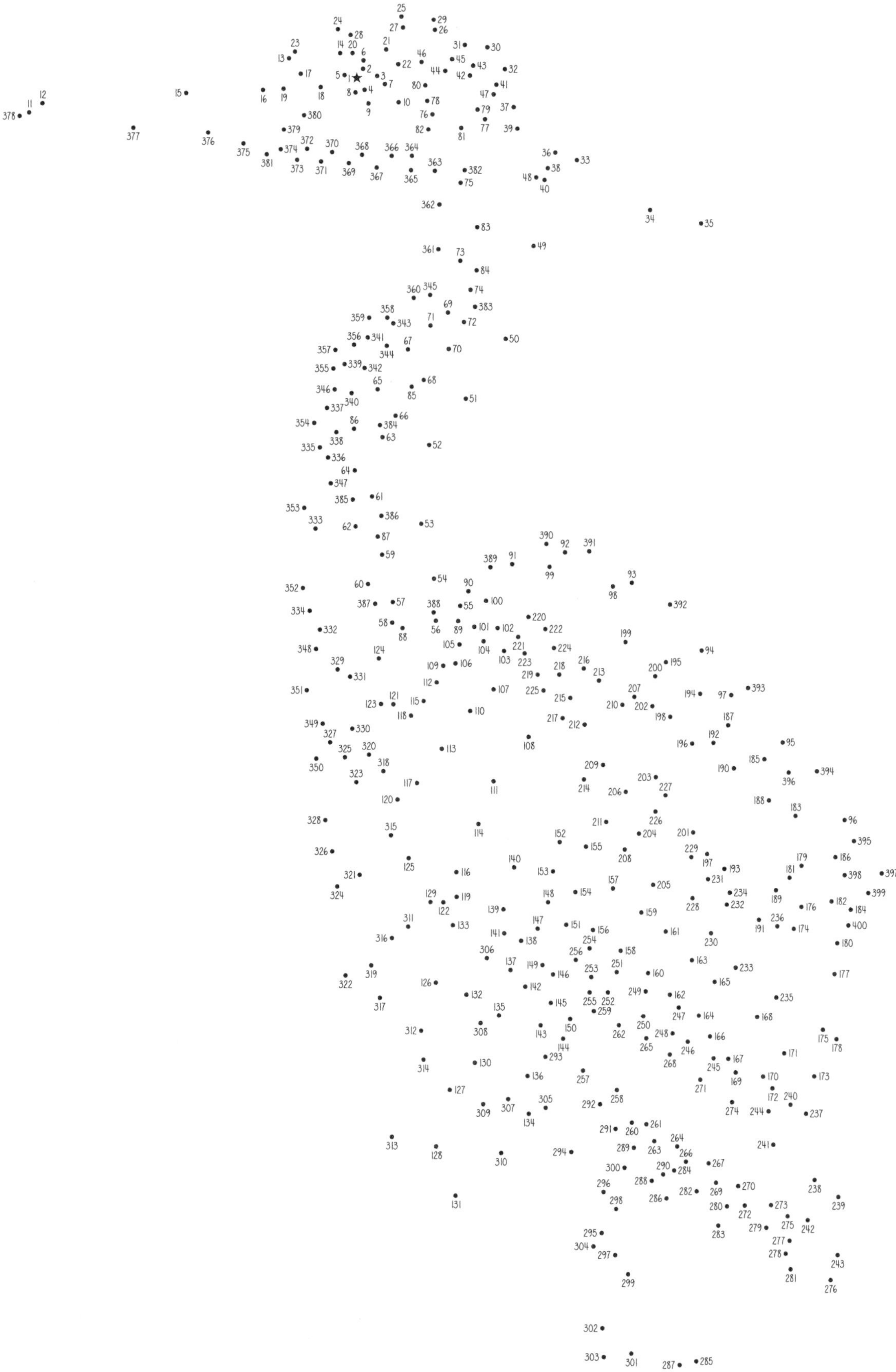

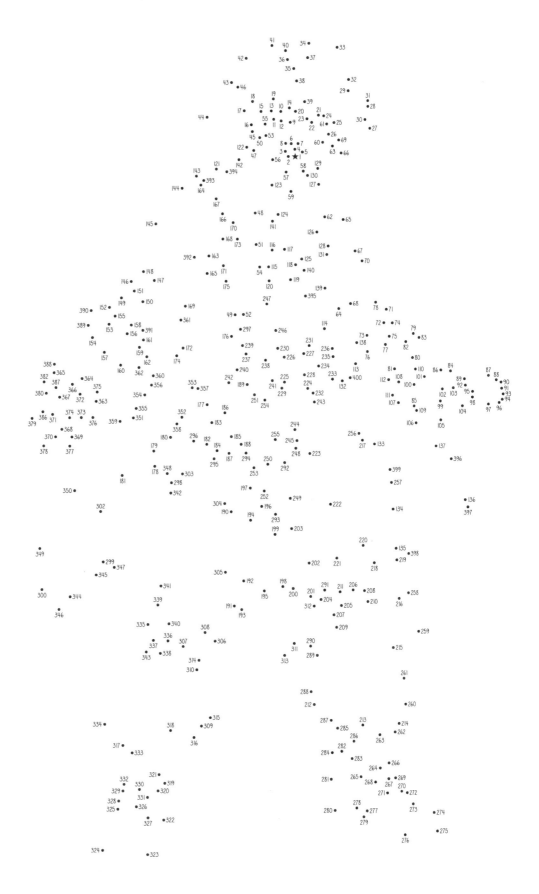

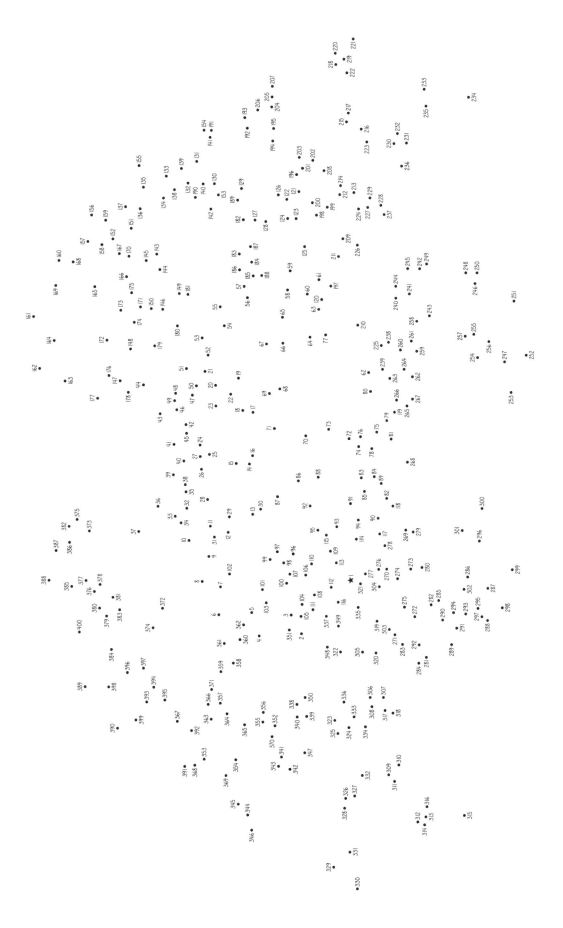

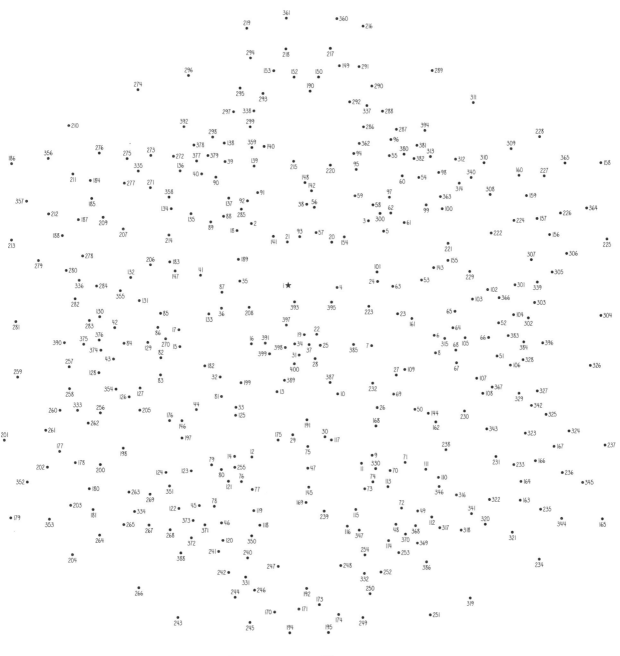

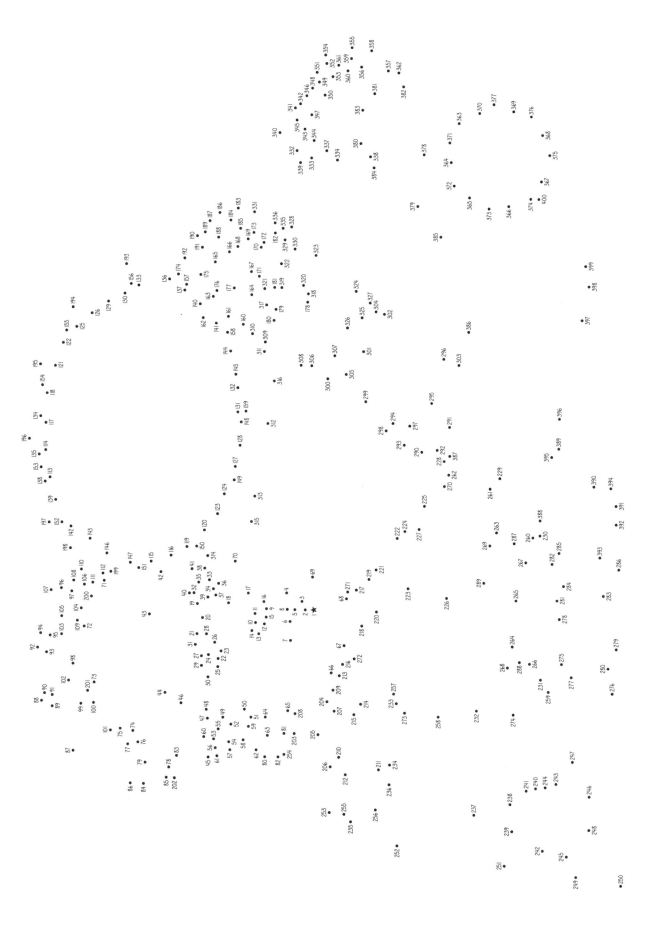

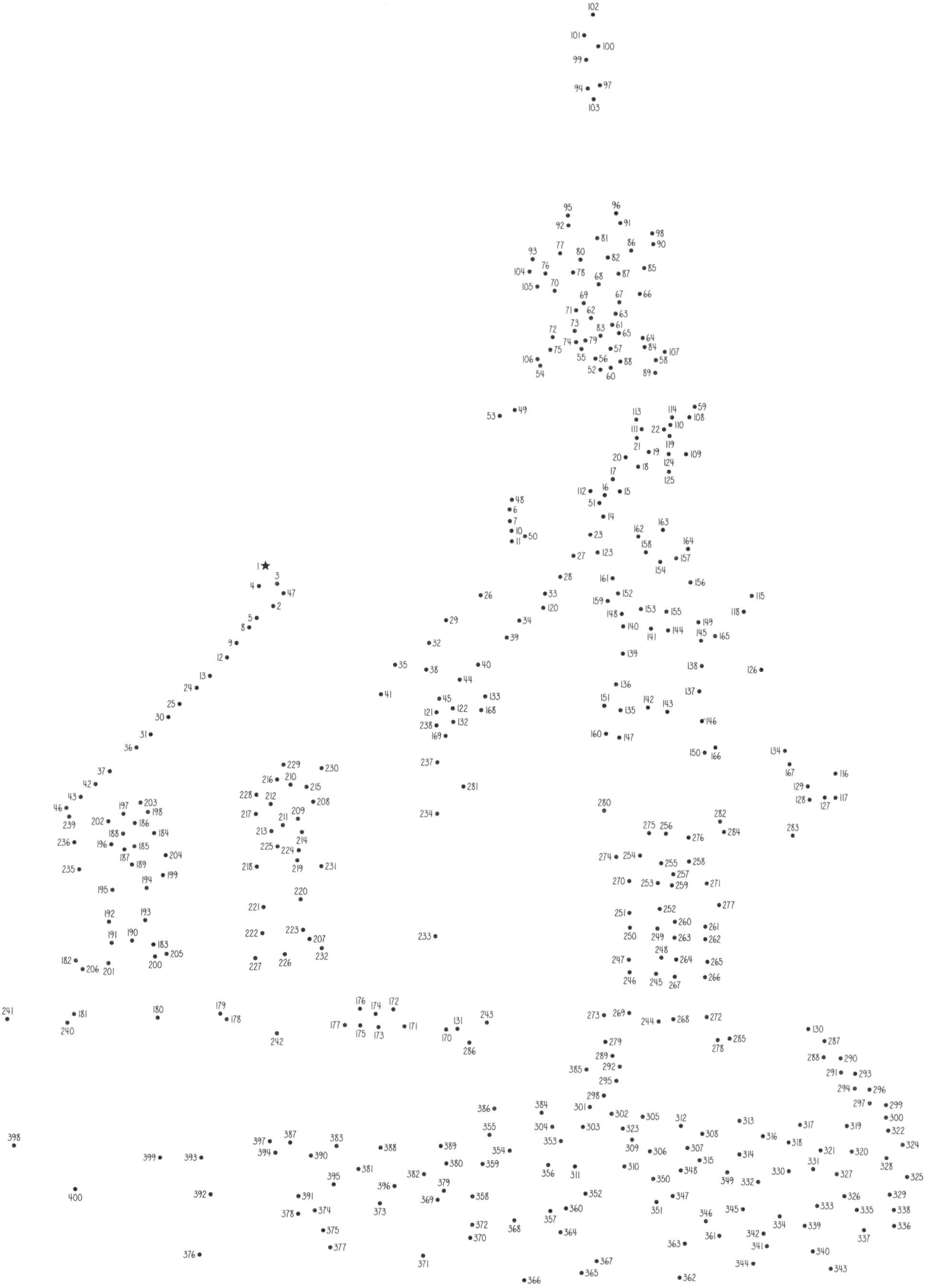

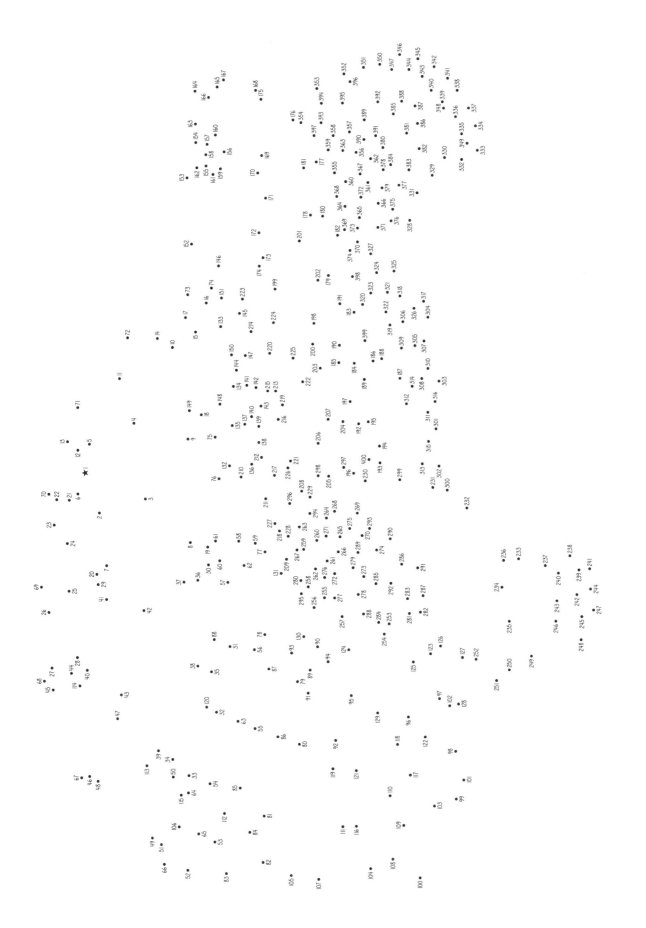

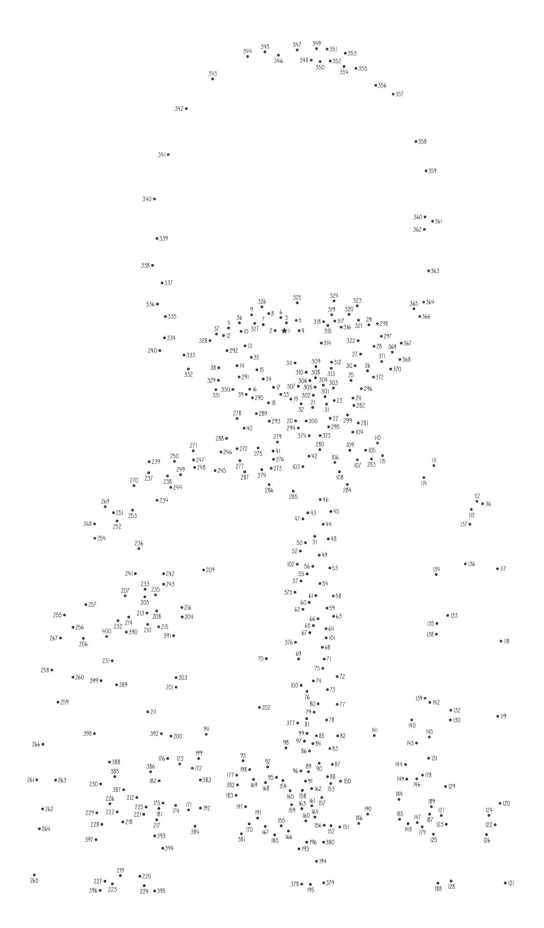

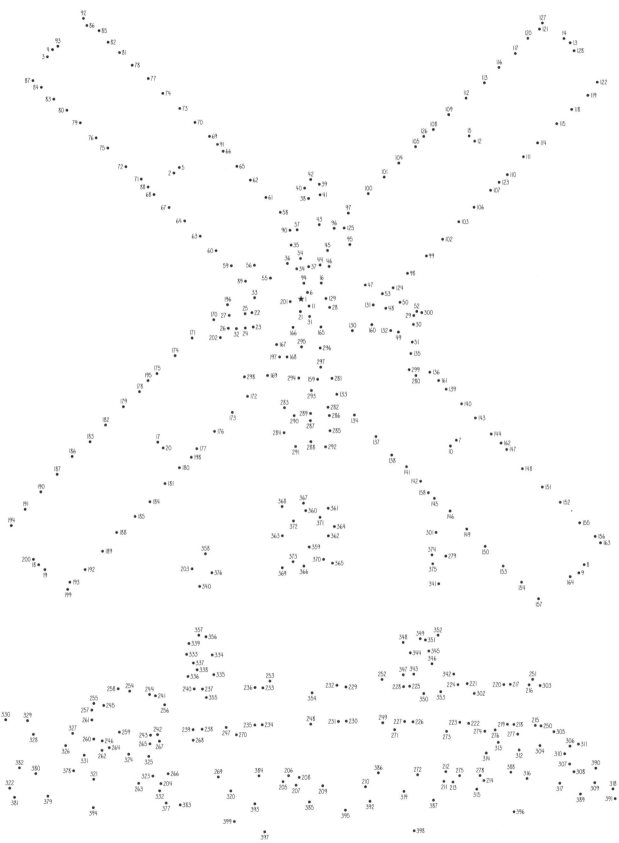

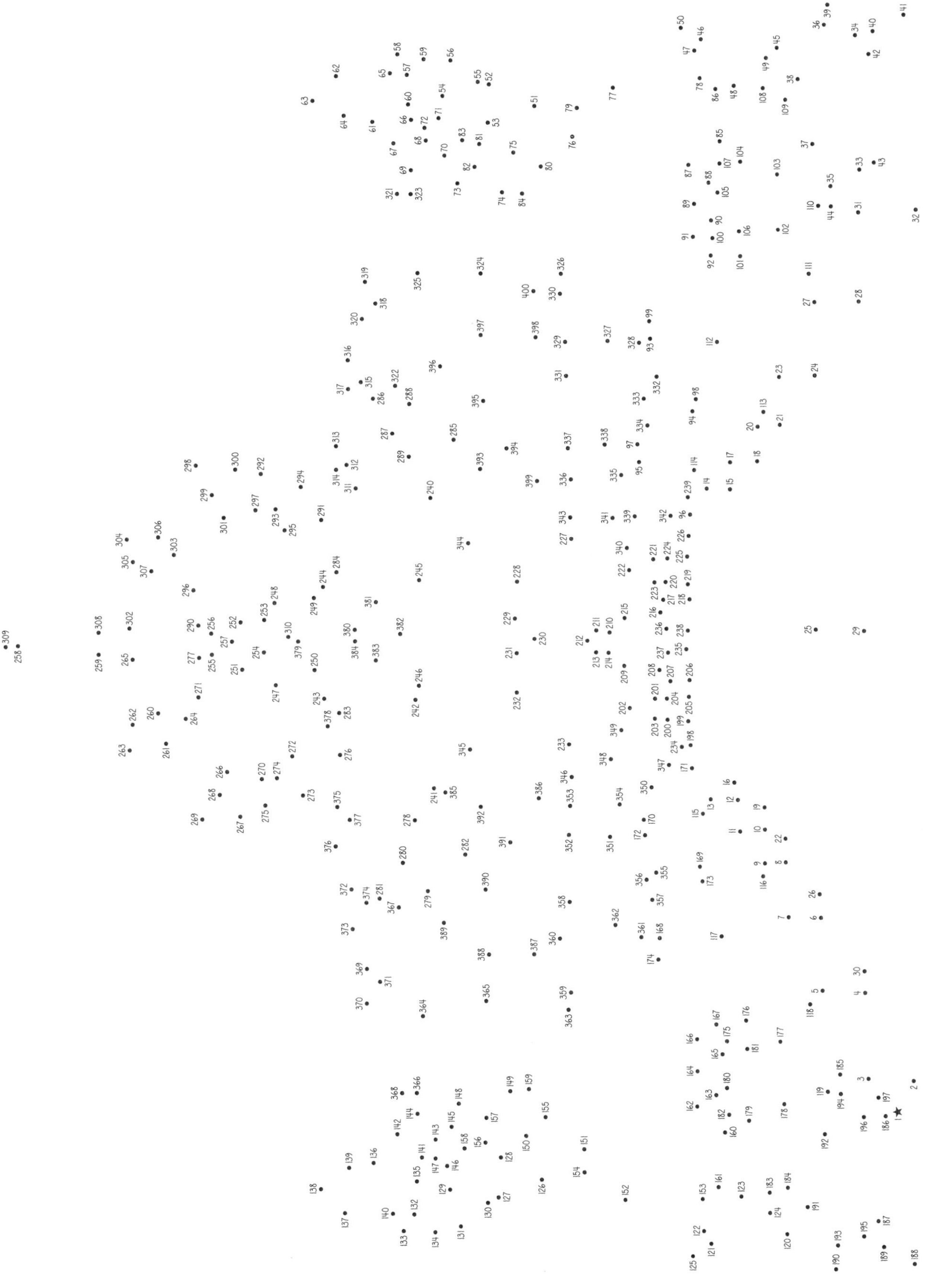

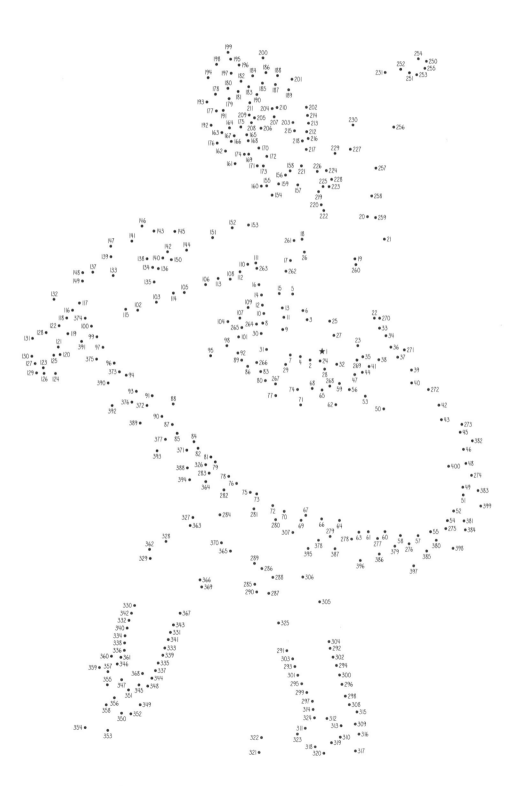

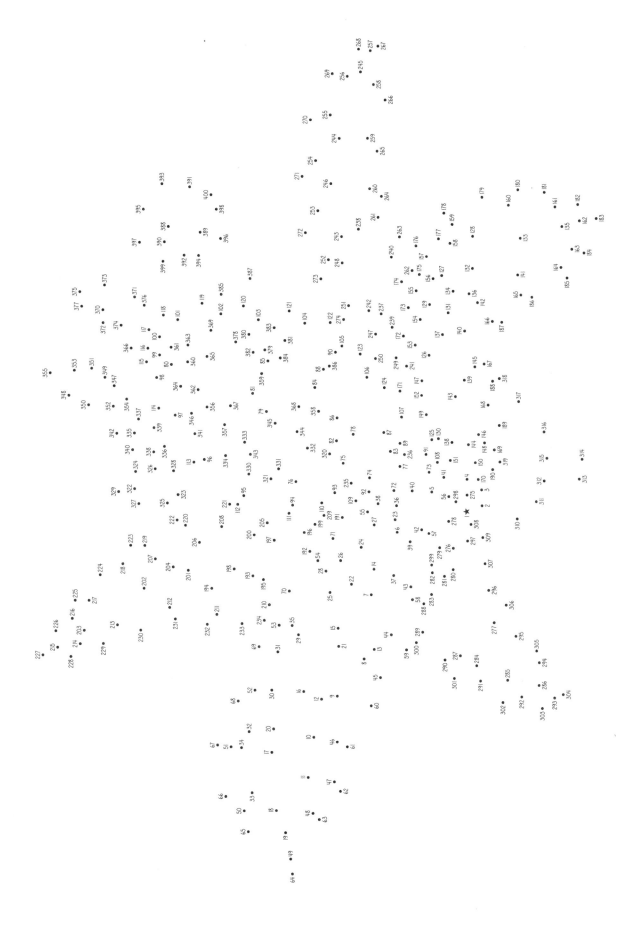

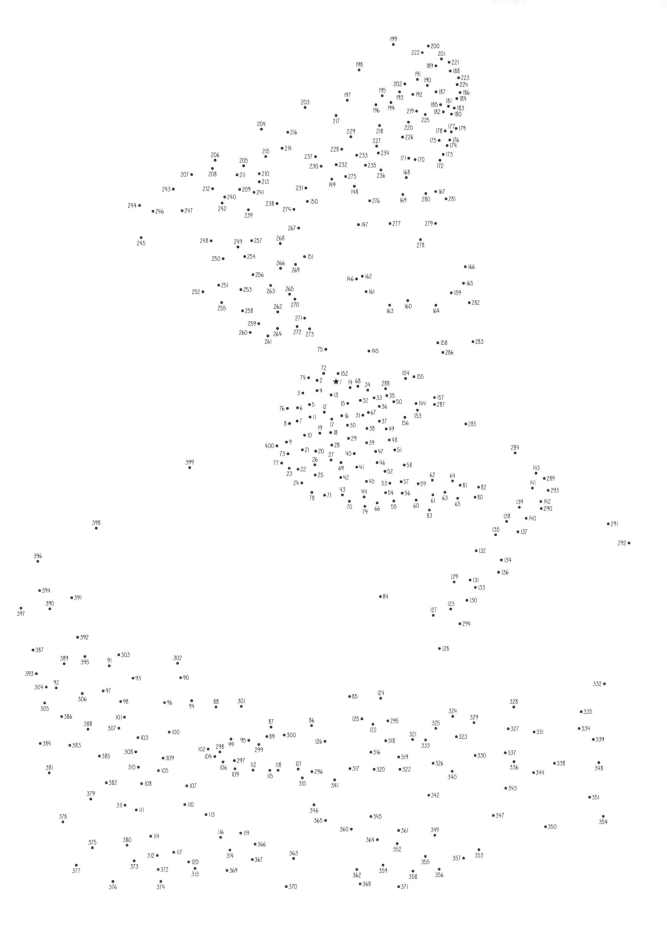

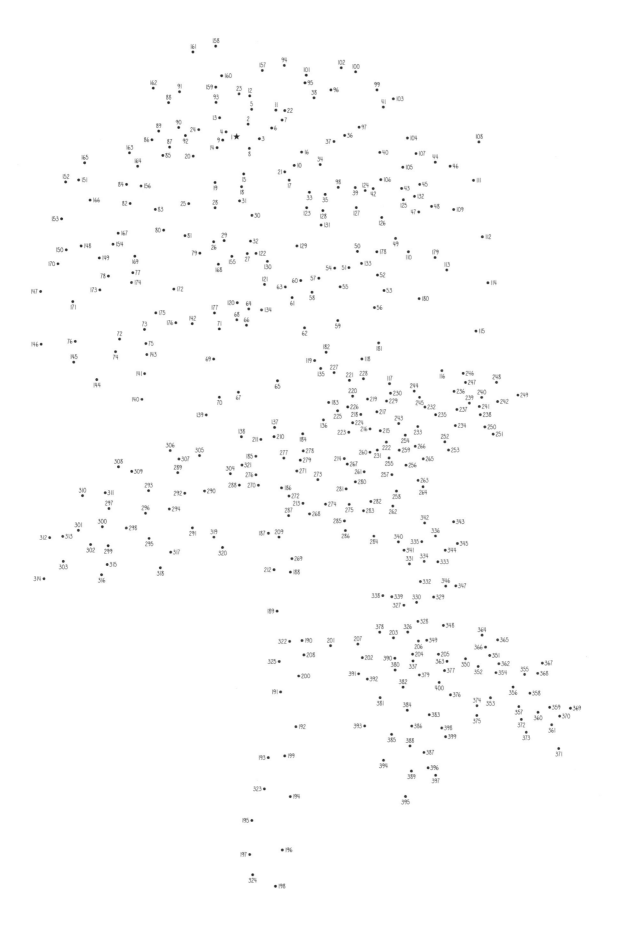

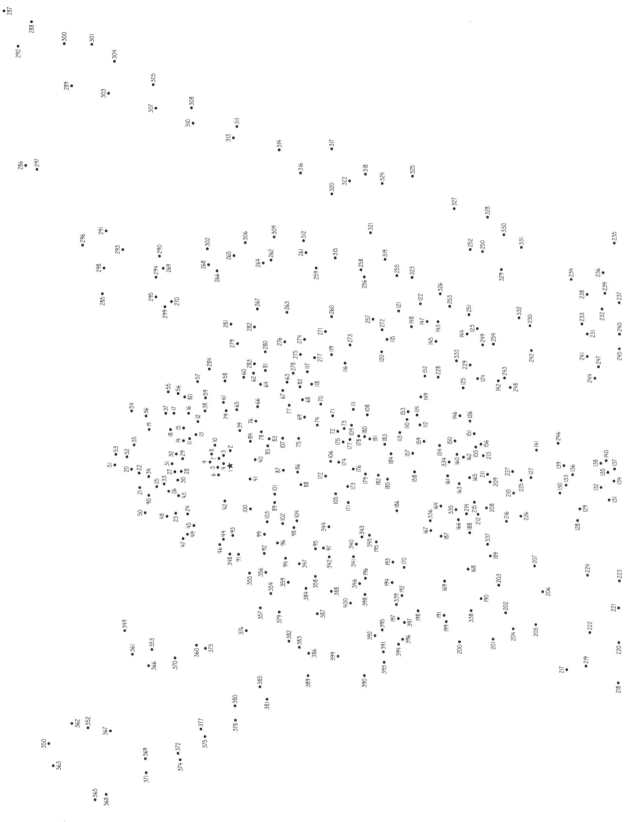

Thanks

A special thank you to my wonderful husband Lewis
for your constant help and support.